Anthony Buckle

Lyrics and Sonnets of Northern Lands

Anthony Buckle

Lyrics and Sonnets of Northern Lands

ISBN/EAN: 9783744797542

Printed in Europe, USA, Canada, Australia, Japan

Cover: Foto ©Thomas Meinert / pixelio.de

More available books at **www.hansebooks.com**

Lyrics and Sonnets

OF

Northern Lands.

BY

A. BUCKLE, B.A.,

Author of "Yorkshire Sonnets and Etchings," &c.

Illustrated with Etchings and Mezzotints,
BY THE AUTHOR.

LEEDS:
RICHARD JACKSON, COMMERCIAL STREET.
1889.

DEDICATED

BY SPECIAL PERMISSION

TO

HER ROYAL HIGHNESS

THE PRINCESS OF WALES.

TO

Her Royal Highness
The Princess of Wales.

PRINCESS, belov'd for kindly deeds,
  Your praise I venture not to sing;
From Denmark's fair poetic fields
  Some simple flowers I only bring,
Which, if they win your gracious smile,
  Will beam as if refresh'd with dew,
And fragrance yield in this our Isle,
  As in the land where first they grew.

This Edition is limited to 300 *Copies, of which this is Number* 137.

PREFACE.

THE formation of very delightful friendships in Denmark and Norway turned my attention to their literature, which, with some knowledge of German, soon yielded me much pleasure. The lyrics of these languages were to me so much in harmony with my own feelings, that the temptation to translate them proved irresistible. Shelley says: "The sweetest songs are those which tell of saddest thought;" and this feature will be found abundantly illustrated in the specimens I offer; while I think other lyric qualities will not be missing. I have tried to preserve in the translations both spirit and form. None but those who have tried to translate poems know how far short the best translations often fall of the full force of the original. These efforts do not pretend to be exceptions in this respect.

The concluding Lyrics, Roundels, and Sonnets are mostly occasional pieces, and must speak for themselves.

A. BUCKLE.

Manor House, York.

CONTENTS.

Part 1.—From the Norwegian.

FROM J. S. C. WELHAVEN:
    The Fairies' whisper - - - - - - - 17
    The Bowstring - - - - - - - 19
    Alluring Sounds - - - - - - - 21
    A Spring Night - - - - - - - 23
H. IBSEN:
    Light-fear - - - - - - - 25
    The Butterfly - - - - - - - 27
ANDREAS MUNCH:
    The joy of sorrow - - - - - - 28
    Sabbath Rest - - - - - - - 29
B. BJÖRNSON:
    The Tryst - - - - - - - 31
    Hidden Love - - - - - - - 33
THEODOR KJERULF:
    Know'st thou the way? - - - - - 34
    Sonnet - - - - - - - 35
P. A. JENSEN:
    The Sea - - - - - - - 36
JÖRGEN MOE:
    God has taken care of it - - - - - 37
    The quenched Light - - - - - - 39
H. A. BJERREGAARD:
    The Bard amidst the ruins - - - - 41
ANONYMOUS:
    The tear - - - - - - - 45
    Memory - - - - - - 47

Part 2.—From the Danish.

OEHLENSCHLÄGER:
    The Moon in Twilight - - - - 51
    Spring - - - - - - 53

ST. ST. BLICHER:
    To Sorrow - - - - - - 56
    The Vale of Love - - - - - 58

C. K. F. MOLBECH:
    To the Woods! - - - - - 61

HOSTRUP:
    The Lark - - - - - - 63

HEDE VIG:
    The Lark - - - - - - 66

HOEGH-GULDBERG:
    The peaceful Land - - - - 67

H. V. KAALUND:
    Restless Longing - - - - - 69

C. PLOUG:
    Wilt thou love me? - - - - - 71

CHRISTIAN WILSTER:
    Day and Evening - - - - 73

ERICA:
    The white Lychnis - - - - 75

B. S. INGEMANN:
    The Wanderer - - - - - 78

Part 3.—Lyrics, Roundels, and Sonnets.

LYRICS:
    A Spring Evening - - - - 83
    The Poppies - - - - - 85

ROUNDELS:
- Life's Measure - 86
- "Like one of these" - 87
- Rest - 88
- The Marriage Bells - 89

SONNETS:
- Home.—I. Youth - 90
-   „ II. Manhood - 91
-   „ III. Old Age - 92
- The Labourer's Hire - 93
- "They supposed they should have received more" 94
- Saturday Evening - 95
- Dante's "Vita Nuova" - 96
- Durham Cathedral - 97
- To the primrose - 98
- The Silver Wedding - 99
- Constancy - 100
- Voices of the Sea - 101
- Absence - 102
- "To-day shalt thou be with Me," &c. - 103
- Easter Even - 104
- Easter Day - 105
- By the Sea Shore - 106
- Called away - 107
- To the Departed - 108
- Christmas - 109
- The Christmas Bells - 110
- Morning - 111
- John Bunyan - 112
- In Memoriam - 113
- The Rising Moon - 114
- Love's Feast - 115

LIST OF ILLUSTRATIONS.

1. In St. Hilda's, Whitby - - - - frontispiece
2. On the Ure - - - - - page 25
3. Runswick Bay (mezzotint) - - - ,, 37
4. Etty's Tomb, St. Mary's Abbey, York ,, 41
5. Moonlit Vale (mezzotint) - - - ,, 51
6. Bishopthorpe Lane - - - - ,, 63
7. Bridlington Quay - - - - ,, 73
8. Kirkham Bridge - - ,, 87
9. Village Church - - - - - ,, 95
10. Coast, Scarbro' (mezzotint) - - - ,, 101
11. Coast, Whitby - - - - ,, 106
12. Richmond, Yorkshire - - - - ,, 111

PART I.

From the Norwegian.

THE FAIRIES' WHISPER.

(After J. S. C. Welhaven.)

1807-1873.

IT is a gladsome summer day,
   The woods with flowerets sweet are gay,
     And rustlings of the leaves;
The fairies flit in dusky shade,
And whisper, "Come into our glade
     Beneath our pleasant eaves."

"It is so mild, it is so still,
   With flowers thy bosom thou may'st fill
     Of scent and beauty rare;
Or if thou would'st thine hours beguile
With pleasant dreams, O rest awhile
     On mossy couch so fair."

I wander on by voices led,
Thro' shady paths I softly tread
     The wood's recess amid;
And there I hear the voice again
Of fairies in a sweet refrain,
     Behind the tree stems hid.

They seem at each footstep to say,
"Where hast thou left thy love to-day,
   That she is not with thee?
There, by the tree, is room for two,
A veil of shadows over you
   Would fall, and none could see."

"She is so fair, she is so sweet,
On summer nights we often meet
   Her pleasing dreams to weave;
And here could she, if thou didst plead,
Blushing and glad, give thee the mead
   Thy heart would fain receive."

How sweet her praise! now wakes again
My secret, deep, and lasting pain
   In this all peaceful grove.
My mouth is closed, my yoke I feel;
No resting place, no balm to heal
   This heart with wound of love.

THE BOW-STRING.

(After J. S. C. Welhaven.)

YOUNG Thorarin, the archer,
   Unto the war would hie,
That he might win some booty rare
His tent to deck, where skin of bear
   Upon the floor did lie.

But first he sought the woodland
   Where birches thick were set;
For there, while birds did sweetly sing,
Was caught the archer's heart one spring
   In Freia's secret net.

There came the Jarl's fair daughter
   To bid a sweet farewell;
How soft that eve the fairies dance,
The lengthening shades their joy enhance
   As they their pledges tell.

Around her brow fair roses
   And clover leaves were bound;
Said he, "O, give me these, I pray,
To tell of thee in danger's day,
   While smites the sword around."

Said she, "'Mid strife and battle
  These beauties of the spring
Will fade, so for thy safety take
What charm and weapon both will make,
  A sure and strong bow-string."

Then on a hillock sat she,
  And shore her locks of gold,
That in the setting sun shone bright,
And to his bow she bound them tight,
  And said, "Now that will hold:

"How much thy bow thou usest
  In battle's fearful rout,
This string will ever supple be,
And firm and strong full constantly,
  Like heart's faith will hold out."

Brave Thorarin, the archer,
  When past the parting pang,
All fearless to the battle went;
And gladness to his heart oft sent
  The bow-string's joyous clang.

ALLURING SOUNDS.

(AFTER J. S. C. WELHAVEN.)

A BIRD flew o'er the fir trees high,
　　Singing the songs of long ago;
They drew me on alluringly
By shady woodland paths to go;
I wander'd to the hidden spring
Where timid deer their thirst could slake,
And still I heard alluring sing
The birds their sweetest echoes make;
　　　Tirilill teen,
Far, far in woods green.

I stood amid the birchen vale,
Where noonday rays gave mellow light,
The dewdrops sparkled in the dale,
The cliffs on high like gold shone bright;
The waving trees made pleasant sound,
Like nestling wings that fluttered nigh;
I heard thro' all the woods around,
The alluring tones that seem'd to cry
　　　Tirilill teen,
Far, far in woods green.

A shaded path led far away
Where birds built homes among the trees,
And each one sang the livelong day
As if they would my heart appease.
If now the place no more I gain,
The deep alluring tones I know,
Which summer long with sweet refrain
Still call me where I oft would go;
    Tirilill teen,
Far, far in woods green.

A SPRING NIGHT.

(After Welhaven.)

THE spring night cool and still
　　Sheds peace on dale and hill;
The brooklet in the glade
Sings a sweet serenade;
Fairies flying,
Deeply sighing
For the beauteous lily's shade.

The silver'd ridge on high
Tells that the moon is nigh;
While o'er the tree-tops go
The clouds like swans of snow;
Soon gentle beams
In mildest gleams
Shine o'er the beauties here below.

Close not thine eye to-night,
But in thy memory's light
Run o'er her pages clear,
As lone thou sittest here;
While forms flit by
All silently
Among the silver'd branches near.

Hark! how these whispers tell
Of dreams thou lovest well!
See, now they bring again
The times that made thee fain;
O, list awhile,
They will beguile
And ease thy yearning heart's deep pain.

LIGHT-FEAR.

(H. Ibsen, 1825.)

IN boyhood's time of long ago
   No fear possessed my mind,
To chatter all the daylight through
   Amidst my happy kind.

But when the shades of even
   Fell, over dale and hill,
Dark forms from many a story
   My mind with fears would fill.

And when my eye was closed,
   They peopled oft my dream,
And all my courage vanish'd
   Till morning's welcome beam.

But now all that is changed,
   With other things beside:
My fear comes now with daylight
   And life's incoming tide.

Now it is day's dark phantoms,
   And all the din of life,
That raise perplexing riddles
   To fill my heart with strife.

And now I must betake me
　To hide 'neath night's veil cold,
When all my longings waken
　As daring as of old.

Nor sea nor flame affright me,
　I fly like hawk on prey—
Forget all grief and sorrow
　Until the morning grey.

Should night's defence be wanting,
　I feel in direst need,
And work then undertaken
　Will be but dark indeed.

THE BUTTERFLY.
(H. Ibsen.)

He:

AGNES, my pretty butterfly,
    To catch thee my heart longs;
I weave a net with meshes small,
    The meshes are my songs.

She:

Am I a pretty butterfly?
    My sweets then let me sip;
And thou art kind and lovest play,
    Chase me, but let me slip.

He:

Agnes, my pretty butterfly,
    My net is now complete;
Thy flitting can help thee no more,
    Soon thou art caught, my sweet.

She:

Am I a pretty butterfly
    That joy and brightness brings?
If caught within thy cunning net,
    O, spare my fragile wings.

He:

Ah, yes! I'll take thee in my hand,
    And shut thee in my heart,
Where thou may'st play the whole day long,
    With no wish to depart.

THE JOY OF SORROW.
(After Andreas Munch, b. 1811.)

MY heart in deepest grief hath toss'd,
    Yet sweet this comfort still doth fall:
" 'Tis better to have lov'd and lost
Than never to have lov'd at all."*

But not indifference I sought
To soothe my grief, or dull my pain,
For what hath life to that one brought
Who in love's arms hath never lain?

For love, heaven's joys will ever sing,
While riches oft, alas! deceive;
What comfort many a lonely eve
Can memory to my sad heart bring!

How sweet she comes, and tells my heart
Of happy days long since gone by,
Till all earth's shadows vain depart,
And I long for the meeting nigh.

Yes, joy may come at sorrow's cost,
Love's words will still in comfort fall:
" 'Tis better to have lov'd and lost
Than never to have lov'd at all."

---

* The original of this couplet is:
    " Det er bedre at have elsket og tabt
    End aldrig at have elsket en gang."

SABBATH - REST.

(Andreas Munch)

SABBATH-REST!
O, to keep without alloy
In my breast
This heaven's joy,
When it falls so sweet and cheery
On my weary,
Poor heart;
Like a summer rain that blesses
The dry earth, and with caresses
From it takes the long drought's smart.

Sabbath-rest!
Thine is no death's heavy stillness,
Deep depressed,
Nor cheerlessness
Of lone places still and sad.
Thou dost glad
With sweet food
My worn spirit, and like spring,
Refresh'd, I mount on thy wing
To the Giver of all good.

Sabbath-rest!
Now hath filled my longing heart,
Thy peace so blest;
And no smart
Nor earth's din can me molest,
Nor its care
Again ensnare,
Nor disturb this joy supernal
In my soul, for peace eternal
Is thy source, O Sabbath-rest!

THE TRYST.

(After B. Bjornsen, b. 1832.)

THE evening is still,
 Strange doubts my heart fill,
Silence reigns o'er the great deep;
Thoughts all unrestful,
Listening, questful,
Will she her promised tryst keep?

Winter is dreaming,
Fair stars are beaming
Like flowrets in the green lane,
Of summer telling,
Love and joys welling;
May she not meet me again?

The sea fast in ice-band
Lies still by the cold strand,
Longing its bonds to break through;
Not a ship sailing,
Thoughts unavailing;
O, for our meeting—we two!

Wildly the snow flies,
And like soft down lies
In the dark wood there below;
Beasts away creeping,
Dark shadows sleeping;
Was that thy footstep? Ah, no!

Courage doth fail thee,
What can avail thee?
Though longing, bewitched thou dost stay;
Fain would I grasp thee,
In these arms clasp thee,
Where thou dost dream time away.

HIDDEN LOVE.

(BJÖRNSEN.)

ALL restless he wandered around,
All gaily she danc'd o'er the ground
With laughter and chat,
To this one and that;
His heart was nigh breaking to view it,
And yet was there no one who knew it.

She went by the barn at the eve,
He came there to take his last leave!
Poor heart! all forlorn
To weep and to mourn;
Yea, deep in her heart did she rue it,
And yet was there no one who knew it.

How slow seem'd the time to pass o'er!
He turn'd to his lode-star once more:
But she lay at rest,
Calm peace fill'd her breast;
Yet still she was true to him through it,
And yet was there no one who knew it.

KNOW'ST THOU THE WAY?

(THEODOR KJERÙLF, b. 1825.)

O LITTLE bird! know'st thou the way
   Which is unknown to me?
How swift thou flewest at break of day,
   With heart all full of glee!

Around thy neck my message tied,
   Full of my longing mind;
Thy speed the sailor has outvied,
   Thou waitest for no wind.

No sweet reply can I get now;
   No word to ease my pain;
I know not when, I know not how,
   Or if we meet again.

O might that be, what gladness then!
   I'd sing, sweet bird, like thee;
O come and tell me of the when
   That happy time shall be.

SONNET.

(Theodor Kjerùlf.)

I SEE thee when I wake and when I dream,
   For when across the beauteous meads I gaze,
   Mysterious in the shimmering noontide haze,
   O'er all like fragrance sweet thy face doth beam.
Then to my heart the blood in fullest stream
   Will rush; until I sink in deep amaze:
   How sweet and bitter is the cup I raise
   To drink, ah, none indeed can truly deem!
How oft like one intoxicate I wake,
   And feel the scalding tears upon my cheek,
   And brood for long upon my throes of pain!
O is it but a dream, unreal and vain,
   Or are these memories, vibrations weak
   Of broken strings, that once did music make?

THE SEA.

(P. A. Jensen, 1812–1867.)

'NEATH darkness rolling,
    Wild waves are foaming,
Storm winds are howling
Like lost spirits roaming:
The storm-fiend, as though madly hurl'd,
    Is snorting on its wide-spread wings,
    While all around it wildly flings
Strange fright upon a troubl'd world.

But dost thou not know
Amidst all thy fright,
There raves not below
The storm's dreadful might?
Yes; there its hoarsest howlings cease,
    In halls of fairest sapphire blue,
    'Mid pearls and corals, far below,
'Neath all earth's tempests, there is Peace.

GOD HAS TAKEN CARE OF IT.
(Jörgen Moe, 1813-1881)

I HAVE a child of four years old,
    A little maiden fair,
Her worth to me can ne'er be told,
    Dark eyes and nut-brown hair.

She stood and gazed in joyous mood
    Through the clear window-pane;
The sun was setting o'er the wood
    With glowing royal train.

Still brighter shone his grand display,
    New beauties still unfold;
The purple clouds all peaceful lay,
    Their edges decked with gold.

The little maid in silence stood
    Entrancèd with the sight,
As if into her soul she would
    Drink in the roseate light.

No word she spake, but gazed on
    With look of fixed intent,
Until the pageant all was gone,
    And the last beams were spent.

Then turn'd with look of sad dismay,
   And with a gentle sigh,
"Now God has put them all away,"
   Said she, with downcast eye.

Ah, yes! my child, so will it be,
   Yea, many and many a time,
When with thy soul's eye thou dost see
   God's glory so sublime.

Again thou'lt see it pass away
   And in the dark be lost,
Nor faintest beam thy gaze repay,
   Where late it glow'd the most.

But in thy mind the truth inlay,
   Which just now thy heart spake;
For "God doth put it all away,"
   But only for thy sake.

Thus Heaven hides oft its glories bright
   From its own children's eyes,
One day to glad in fuller light,
   Their hearts with blest surprise.

THE QUENCHED LIGHT.

MY light is quench'd, my own young bride,
    Thou wast my altar flame;
O God, from Thee I wander wide,
    From whom her sweet love came.

Dark on the wreck I sit again,
    The tossing waves sweep o'er;
For break of day I sigh in vain,
    Night covers sea and shore.

And darkness all my soul doth fill,
    While quenchèd is thy light;
No ray of joy my grief doth still,
    Whilst thou glad'st not my sight.

Earth has no voice of power to reach
    This listening ear of mine,
That longs to catch in gentle speech
    Some precious word of thine.

And while I gaze not on thy face,
　Pure lily bright and fair,
The sun can beautify no place,
　For thou, love, art not there.

But if on earth, sweet summer flower,
　I gaze on thee no more,
At length I know, in God's good hour,
　My life's night will be o'er.

THE BARD AMIDST THE RUINS.

(H. A. BJERREGAARD, 1792-1842.)

DARKLY stood the ruin'd castle,
   In the stillness of the night,
While the peaceful stars of heaven
   Shed o'er it their glimmering light.

Round were scatter'd broken fragments
   Of the beauteous carved stone,
And between the shatter'd pillars
   Sat a harper, sad and lone.

By his breast his harp he rested,
   O'er its strings with sad caress
Pass'd his wither'd hands, all trembling,
   Till it spoke as in distress.

Louder grew the tones of wailing,
   As a strange and powerful clang
Sounded on the quiet night-air,
   And to it the harper sang:—

"Fingers stiff and eyes all weary,
   Sits the singer lone and old,
While above, the stars of heaven
   Shed their beams so bright and cold.

"Soon this trembling heart is stilled,
   Soon these eyes shall lose their light;
Come then, bard, and sing thy last song
   In the still and peaceful night.

"Soon the day of life is ended,
   With death's starry night at hand;
What I sought hath not been missing,
   Now to go, I ready stand.

"I can die, for I have lived,
   Lov'd, and sung, and suffer'd too;
Something in my life effected,
   Many a fight have battl'd through.

"Tones of heaven brought to earthward,
   On my harp's poor trembling string;
Passions waked and restrained,
   Heighten'd joy, taught grief to sing

"Hearts have I oft set to bleeding,
   Swell with joy, or thrill with pain;
Hearts have I oft set to glowing
   With the bliss of hope again.

"I have clasp'd a darling maiden,
    Clasp'd in faith and truth a friend;
They are gone, and now the harper
    Calmly waits the appointed end.

"Cease, O heart of mine, thy beatings;
    Thou hast throbb'd to many a sigh;
Leave behind earth's joys and sorrows,
    Mount to star-crowds far on high.

"Fare thee well, thou heaven above me!
    Fare thee well, thou beauteous earth!
Fare ye well, ye flowery meadows!
    Fare ye well, ye birds of mirth!

"Fare ye well, too, cares and sorrows!
    Soon is mute the harper's voice,
For his last time, now the old bard
    In his swan-song can rejoice.

"Yet one wish alone remaineth!
    Only one ere life hath pass'd:
That amidst these ancient ruins
    He may find his grave at last.

"Here it would be well to slumber,
    Here a bard might rest content,
For no art of man could raise him
    Such a glorious monument."

As the last tones died away,
   Crash'd the thunder peal around,
Dash'd the pillars o'er the singer,
   Who his wish'd-for grave hath found.

Thus above his worn-out body
   Rise aloft the sculptur'd stones,
And at night, from underneath them,
   Oft are heard a harp's strange tones.

THE TEAR.

GREAT is friendship's might,
  Sweet is love's true plight,
And the joys they give our life endear;
  But not friendship's glance,
  Nor looks that hearts entrance,
But devotion's pledge is a tear.

  Trust no flatterer's smile
  Who would with lying guile,
Gain for selfish ends thy willing ear;
  But the eye so true,
  Where the soul looks through
And is shining bright in a tear.

  Warrior bold in fight
  Bravely for the right,
Battle's danger sees without a fear;
  Yet his tender heart
  Feels for foe a smart,
And bathes his wound with a tear.

But when war is o'er,
And in peace once more
He can lay aside the wounding spear;
Then in love's embrace,
From that smiling face
He can kiss away the trembling tear.

Sailor brave and free,
When the raging sea
Seems to tell him death is near,
And that threatening wave
Soon may be his grave,
Thinks of his dear home with a tear.

When comes that blest release
Which calls the soul to peace,
And to meetings with the lost and dear;
When by my grave ye stand,
A silent, mourning band,
O then bedew my dust with a tear!

MEMORY.

On winged feet I fled afar,
    Far from each well-known place,
Memory, I thought, would stay her car,
    Nor follow in the race.

Onwards I sped o'er wildest sea,
    On mountain heights I stand;
But in my breast still lurketh she,
    And wields her wounding brand.

On earth is no resistless shield
    To ward her heavy blow;
Wounded I lie on mountain field,
    The unstaunched blood will flow.

PART II.

From the Danish.

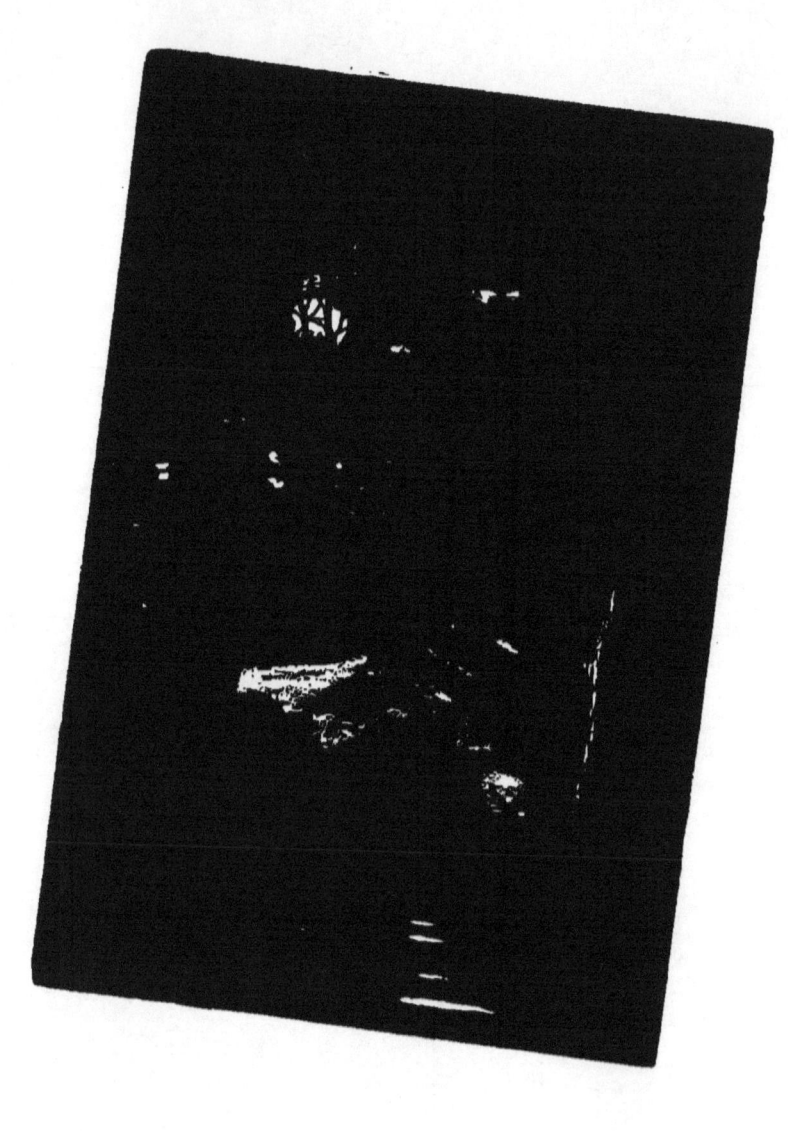

THE MOON IN TWILIGHT.

(OEHLENSCHLÄGER, 1779-1850.)

THE golden star of evening beams,
    But short its stay;
The chill night-air too cold it deems,
So hastes away:
The roseate rays of setting sun
Are its delight,
Him it follows gladly on,
And knows not night.

But gentle love, with hands so fair,
Likes not the sun,
As violet sweet scents the air
When he is gone.
Then calmly shines the moon on high,
Tender and clear,
To show unto these lovers shy
Some bower near.

There bashful love can tell its tale
And none can pry,
Only the moon sees through the veil,
And she is shy;

Of all things the brooklet chatters
Over its sands,
But the strange tongue it utters
None understands.

So gentle youth and maiden fair
Safe can confide,
And nothing shall disturb them there,
Sat side by side:
The moon will not break the spell
Of their pure bliss,
And only the brooklet can tell
Of the fond kiss.

SPRING.

(OEHLENSCHLÄGER.)

GAY spring now is come,
　Fair smiles the green grove,
The nightingale's song
Pours out his heart's love;
And blushing the roses
Stand thick on the tree,
While bright glance the wavelets
O'er the calm sea.

The star of the evening
Beams full of love's joy!
And see the slim maiden
Bewitching and coy.
How light the soft zephyr
That breathes from the west,
Stirs now the bright flowers
That deck her warm breast.

O maiden, sweet maiden,
I've closed now my book;
And on its dull pages
I care not to look;

The light that I found there
Hath passed away.
O come, my beloved,
Why dost thou delay?

Thou art my fair flower,
My zephyr so sweet,
My lily the purest,
My rose all complete;
The nightingale singeth
When evening shades fall;
Thou singest and talkest,
My sweet all in all!

O come and embrace thou
Thy young singer here,
While soundeth his lyre
In tones thrilling clear;
In love's fetters bind him,
So light and so strong,
O haste thee, and give him
A kiss for his song!

See, time stays his swift flight
When bursts forth the spring,
In youth stand the old days
When glad the birds sing.

In thy fond embrace, love,
Naught's wanting for me,
Fawns leap in the woodland,
And naiads in the sea.

Pan stands by the woods there,
A watchful, true wight,
To chase far time's prudence
With terror and fright;
It would kill my fair Dryad,
My rapt'rous embrace,
While mocking my lov'd one
With laughing grimace.

TO SORROW.

(St. St. Blicher, 1782-1848.)

O THOU who silent with thy head bow'd down
    Like broken lily on its stem bent low,
Who round black locks dost wear a thorny crown,
    As joy's pale sister-angel, whom we know,

Dost thou not come, indeed, from heaven above,
    As storm, and rain, and thunder dost thou fall?
Dost thou come from a God of love,
    Like cloud, thy shadow casting over all?

Is there no comfort in thy throbbing pain?
    Hast thou no soothing in thy bitter tears?
Are only sighs thy constant sad refrain?
    In wounded hearts dost thou but stir up fears?

Ah, no! thou givest strength while casting down,
    Thy cup of tears I shall not drink in vain;
I love thee, too, although I fear thy frown;
    My soul's sad friend, console me once again.

Let me embrace thee as my pale, sad bride,
  And find sweet healing 'neath thy sable wing,
While o'er our heads, as we stand side by side,
  Fair stars of hope their gentle radiance fling.

O come, then, as thou wilt, sent from on high,
  And my poor trembling heart with thee shall stay;
Out of darkness thou wilt guide mine eye
  To the light of everlasting day.

THE VALE OF LOVE.

(St. St. Blicher.)

BEHIND some blue mountains there lies a sweet vale,
So lonely, so peaceful, which storms ne'er assail;
There cometh not winter, with frost or with snow,
'Tis spring there for ever, where soft breezes blow.

It smileth for ever; in spring's beauties clad
With sweet-scented flowers it always is glad;
No changes pass over its beauties still new,
By mountains protected it keeps its fair hue.

Around it for shelter stand woods ever green,
With foliage unchanging in brightening sheen,
While sweet woodland songsters in freedom and joy,
In warblings unending find sweetest employ.

From thick-covered rock heights there leap down below
The clearest of waters, 'mid violets to flow;
So softly they glide there, and wind round and round,
As though they would never flow from so fair ground.

But in this fair valley there lieth conceal'd
A cottage, the neatest to eye e'er reveal'd;
By thick groves surrounded before and behind,
Its straw-cover'd roofing you scarcely can find.

But in the bright sunset its windows small shine
And beam as with gladness two sweet laughing eyne;
While 'midst the bright roses its white walls are seen,
Or in the clear brooklet reflected serene.

And here, by the brooklet, 'mid roses there dwell,
Unseen by the world's eye, as monk in his cell,
Two lovers, whose bosoms are filled but with love,
Whose voices sound soft as the cooing of dove.

When morning awakens the bird on its nest,
It findeth her cheek on his bosom at rest;
When even falls gently with all restful charm,
It finds him encircled by her loving arm.

Like two pearly dewdrops, that sparkle with light,
Within some fair flower cup fall down and unite;
As two lovely lilies on single stem grow,
Though twin flowers blooming, like one blossom show.

They care not for time as it comes or it goes,
They count not the days or the year as it flows;
The past or the future, what is it for them?
The present weaves for them its best diadem.

O, tell us, thou singer, where find we that vale,
So lonely, so peaceful, which storms ne'er assail,
Where spring ever bloometh in beauty all drest,
And love ever filleth the lover's fond breast?

It is a bright dream from my far distant spring,
Which o'er me at sixteen spread$ out its fair wing;
But storms then burst o'er me, and mists, alas! rose,
I lost my sweet valley, where lovers repose.

But if ye should find it, fair youth and sweet maid,
That valley where I would for ever have stayed,
With tenderness think of the poet so fain,
Who found the bright valley and lost it again.

TO THE WOODS!

C. K. F. Moldech, 1821.

COME, come, let us fly,
  I and thou, my heart's joy,
Where trees hide the sky
Where comes no annoy;
Let us fly from this place
Where fetters are round us,
In the wood's joyous space
Sweet peace oft hath found us.

Here love finds no rest,
Like a bird hunted down;
In the woods, on my breast
Thou need'st fear no frown.
Busy tongues, prying eyes,
Ever follow us here;
The lone deer's surprise
We there need not fear.

Come, come, let us fly!
I often can hear
'Mid tumult and cry
The wood's soft call clear:

"O, come to my shade
  Where love's joys abide,
  And each flower in the glade
  Blooms fit for a bride.

"For each loving heart
  In my shades will be found
  Some sweet nook apart
  With soft breezes round.
  Why spend your short life,
  So soon gone for aye,
  'Mid trouble and strife?
  O, come, come away."

Come, come, let us fly!
  I and thou, my heart's joy,
  Where trees hide the sky,
  Where comes no annoy;
  For in twilight's rest
  While life doth repose,
  Love can find a safe nest
  And a cure for all woes.

THE LARK.

(HOSTRUP, b. 1818.)

OF what dost thou sing
    Far up in the sky?
Whose praise dost thou tell
As clear thy notes well
From fount never dry?
Has the sun called thee forth
To tune thy sweet lay,
While cold from the north
Blows the wind o'er the bay?

I fly up so high,
I gaze so far round,
Bright summer I see
In gladness and glee
Trip o'er the fair ground;
All over I hear
Sweet rippling of streams;
And visions of fear
Are passing like dreams.

I gaze so far round,
My song is so bright,
Of mists that are scatter'd,
Of meadows bespattered
With red and with white;
Of ships on waves dancing;
Of seeds that are springing;
Of bright days advancing,
And happiness bringing.

Of what dost thou dream
So high in the blue?
Can gladness be there,
Where eagles can tear
Such small birds as you?
Can meadows give pleasure,
Or bright laden trees,
With fruits beyond measure,
Which dark foes may seize?

I climb up so high,
So wide round I gaze,
Above the mists far
I see a clear star,
Foretelling the days
When sleepers awake,
Who slumber'd so deep,
The idle to quake,
The dead soul to weep.

I climb up so high,
I see with delight
The dutiful youth
His parents requite;
The sayings of home
Still guiding his way,
Where'er he may roam,
Still cheering his day.

I gaze so far round,
My song is so glad,
With fountains clear leaping
With birds in safe keeping
And nothing seems sad;
With peace that is nearing,
With great deeds and song,
No rushing storm fearing
The bright summer long.

THE LARK.
(Hede Vig.)

NO shelter needs this songster dear
In tree or bush, but without fear,
In meadow or amidst the heather,
It builds its nest in sweet spring weather.

But not what doth to earth belong
It seeks, and so its trilling song
It pours in fullest strain, as higher
Aloft its flight is heaven nigher.

More than all other songsters bright
It seeks the blue of heaven's height,
For there above it finds no sadness,
While singing turns its care to gladness.

For there is power in its clear song,
Which oft we've felt both sweet and strong;
Yes, in those gladsome tones "unbidden,"
What blessed comfort oft is hidden!

For heart and eye it draws above,
And hope seems on its wings to move,
As upward mounting in the heaven,
Its song wells forth from morn till even.

THE PEACEFUL LAND.

HÖEGH-GULDBERG, 1771-1852.

THE waves have ceased their tossing,
   The storms are laid to rest,
And scarce a breath is blowing
   O'er ocean's heaving breast!
And in the far-off distance
   A known and lovéd voice,
From land I see by starlight
   Makes all my heart rejoice.

My fatherland! how welcome
   Thy sweet and peaceful shore!
There lovéd ones are gather'd
   To part and mourn no more!
Each place doth touch some heart-chord,
   Each flower bears some sweet name,
All troubles there are vanish'd,
   Forgot all want and shame.

No greener woods or valleys
   And no serener sky,
No warbling songsters sweeter,
   No place can that outvie;

Days undisturbed by longing,
  And trust that knows no bound
Pure hearts and ne'er inconstant
  Can only there be found.

Ye waves, now gently bear me
  To that dear peaceful strand,
Already nears the fair one,
  To lead me safe to land;
I see his torch-light glimmer,
  I know he'll guide me right,
My heart beats with a flutter,
  But with no touch of fright.

Companions of my voyage!
  I bid a last adieu!
And hope one day, safe landed,
  At length to welcome you!
Too bright thy torch! pray shade it!
  I'm dazzled with its glare,
I'll close my eyes a little while
  And open them when there.

RESTLESS LONGING.

H. V. KAALUND, 1818.

BY each aim to which I strive,
　　Longing on life's way;
With each step by which I rise
Still I find no stay;
Scarce I clasp some happy joy
Ere 'tis gone and past,
Wanting, wanting,
Ever wanting to the last.

Rest I find not in my knowledge,
In what I do, or feel,
Time beneath my feet keeps turning
Still its restless wheel;
Scarcely is one foot set down
For a moment's space,
Onward, onward,
Ever onward is the race.

Winged hope I follow after,
With its promise fair,
Still its song deceives me ever,
Always near, yet ever there.
O how sweet comes night's refreshing
For tir'd hand and weary brain,
Then with morning
To awake and strive again.

WILT THOU LOVE ME?

(C. PLOUG, 1813.)

WILT thou love me, when the day is waning,
And its sun is sinking bleak and cold;
When its darkening shadows thickly gather,
And foretell me that its hours are told;
When my foot is weary, and all powerless
Sink my hands upon thy loving breast;
When mine eye in prayer is heavenward turning,
And in need is begging for God's rest?

Wilt thou love me, when what I had promised,
Ne'er, alas! shall I be able to fulfil;
When 'tis plain my heart was all too eager,
And I failed for want of power, not will;
When I'm cast aside like rusty weapon,
Blunt and useless, though once sharp and bright,
And the careless crowd will scarce remember
That I ne'er was backward in the fight?

Wilt thou love me, when these little warblings,
Which from out my full heart gush'd so free,
That they touched other hearts with power,
And first drew thy constant love to me;

When 'mid other songs they are forgotten,
And a younger race heeds them no more;
When they lie upon the shelf neglected,
With the dust of years all covered o'er?

Wilt thou love me, when that rest is gained,
Which this troubled life me never gave;
When the end of all my earnest striving
Seems a mound of earth, an unknown grave?
Wilt thou teach our little ones so truly
Who I was, for what I fought and died?
Wilt thou keep me in thy dearest memory,
Till in peace thou restest by my side?

DAY AND EVENING.

Christian Wilster, 1796–1840.

Day goes slowly to its end,
    Full of toil and care;
Evening is a tender friend,
    With eyes of stars so fair.

Day the thoughts doth scatter wide—
    Far and wide they roam;
Evening calls the heart again
    To its lov'd at home.

Through earth's valleys far and near
    Day casts the eager eye;
Evening turns the prayerful gaze
    To mansions in the sky.

Day is eager and athirst
    Some new gain to win;
Evening hours of peace and rest
    Enjoy what's gathered in.

Day amid its varying scenes
    Sees us laugh and weep;
But the sigh of evening oft
    Stirs a deeper deep.

Daylong wandering far and wide
    The heart can find no rest;
But at even, with sweet song,
    Flies it to its nest.

THE WHITE LYCHNIS.

(ENICA.)

(The White, Corn, or Evening Lychnis *(Lychnis Vespertina)* emits a pleasant odour in the Evening.)

DOWN in the grove a pale star grows,
    Amongst the withered leaves,
And trembling in the bleak winds' play
    A shivering sigh it heaves.

The great eternal starry host
    It gazed upon at night,
Where high in heaven, with silver rays,
    Shone their unfading light.

It dreamt of them the livelong day,
    While lonely there it grew,
And while the summer's beauty far
    Away the rough wind blew.

" Ye beaming stars that peaceful move,
    In sweet and quiet rest,
Beneath that vault, where care nor fear
    Disturbs your joy so blest!

"No raging storm, no sleety blast,
    Nor death's grim form ye know,
While there ye shine, so near God's throne,
    And high above earth's woe!

"I too was made a fair white star,
    A pure and spotless gem,
To tremble but a little while
    Upon this slender stem.

"The first rough wind down in the dust
    My tender crown will lay,
And whirl about 'mid withered leaves
    In its wild heedless play.

"Ye bright and heavenly starry host,
    In the deep blue so high;
The little flower that loves you much
    Will soon be gone for aye!

"Now sinks the sun, and ye come forth,
    And I may gaze once more
On your eternal beauties,
    Ere yet my time is o'er!"

Then spake, as it gazed kindly down,
    The Star of Evening mild:
"O sister sweet, that hid'st thyself,
    Be cheered, my tender child!

"A short and fleeting silver glance
    Our God to thee hath given,
And thou hast raised thy loving eye
    To the star crown of heaven.

"And we, who for our thousand years
    Have held our lofty way,
Think'st thou, fair one, we value much
    Our seeming endless day?

"The song we sing to God on high
    Is that same glorious hymn,
Which with the smallest stars of earth
    We offer up to Him.

"Take comfort, then, for thy short life;
    For one pure tone and clear
Can humbly witness to His might
    On earth as we do here.

"In great creation's harmony,
    Thou, too, dost fill thy part:
Can we do more, my sister dear?
    Then calm thy troubled heart."

THE WANDERER.

B. S. INGEMANN, 1789-1862.

ALL the sky was dull and drear,
    But what cared I!
For my sky shone bright and clear
    In Eliza's eye.

Not a star was to be seen,
    Yet I felt no fear;
For like stars of brightest sheen
    Shone those eyes so dear.

All the way was rough and dark;
    Unheeding wind, or weather,
O'er the roughest path we trudge,
    Joyfully together.

Then the sky again was fair,
    But what cared I!
For I saw no longer there
    My Eliza's eye.

Friendly shone the stars above,
  But joyless was their light;
For in them I could not see
  Her sweet eyes so bright.

Would the sky were dark once more!
  And no star appear!
But give the wanderer back again
  His companion dear.

PART III.

Lyrics, Roundels & Sonnets.

(ORIGINAL.)

Lyrics.

A SPRING EVENING.

THE burdens of the day laid by,
   We wander'd thro' the quiet lane,
As heart in heart my love and I
   Were glad with joys of hope again.

Sweet was the perfum'd breeze of spring
   From whiten'd orchards wafted by,
But sweeter joy to me did bring
   Her gentle, loving presence nigh.

Thou moon, that on our path didst shine
   So fair, as on we saunter'd slow,
Canst thou reveal to heart of mine
   The future that I fain would know?

Ah, no! but in those tender eyes,
   That gaz'd on thee, I fondly trace
A loving sympathy arise,
   Where my glad heart hath found a place.

How restful was the calm of eve!
  The peace beneath the pale moonbeams!
Our hearts forgot one sigh to heave,
  We wander'd as in pleasant dreams.

Fair moon! sweet breeze! all restful calm!
  In life's oft changing joy and care;
May mutual love's blest healing balm
  Our spirits soothe like evening prayer.

THE POPPIES.

MY thoughts were of a sombre turn,
    As thro' the field I took my way;
I mused on all the ills of life,—
    Beclouded heart, beclouded day.

The corn was green, the tender blade
    Gave promise of a harvest fair,
And 'mid the corn in beauty stood
    Some bright red poppies gleaming there.

Then passed the clouds, the sun shone forth
    And filled the land with cheering light;
And 'mid the waving blades of corn,
    Made all the poppies shine more bright.

So in life's anxious cares and toils
    Our Father's love I seem'd to see;
Some little joys to cheer each lot
    He sendeth to us constantly.

With hopeful heart and trusting love
    We'll joyful to our work at morn,
While smiling eyes and loving deeds
    Shine like the poppies 'mid the corn.

Roundels.

I.

LIFE'S MEASURE.

NOT by years, but deeds all bright,
    Wrought 'mid joys and hopes and fears,
We will measure life aright,
    Not by years.

Love, though gazing oft through tears,
Then o'er life shall shed its light,
Dreading not the end that nears,

Nobly striving in the fight,
Till the long'd-for rest appears,
When bliss is measured infinite,
    Not by years.

II.
"LIKE ONE OF THESE."

"LIKE one of these," as here they stand and shine,
Or dance in gladness in the summer's breeze,
Thou canst not deck thyself in silks so fine,
"Like one of these."

But cast aside, O man, ignoble ease,
In self negation rise to heights divine,
Nor seek in life alone the deeds that please.

Thus shall thy very soul herself inshrine
In beauties which the outward eye ne'er sees,
Whose splendours waste not in a sad decline,
"Like one of these."

III.

REST.

A LITTLE rest! O tired and weary heart!
After thy long and seeming bootless quest,
How sweet this balm to heal some bitter smart,—
A little rest!

Ye patient ones, who toil 'mid sighs supprest,
And meekly, lovingly sustain your part,
At length your dreary day sinks in the west:

Then shall be wiped away the tears that start,
His answer meet be given to your request,
When in God's love ye have with Him apart
A little rest!

IV.

THE MARRIAGE BELLS.

THE music of the bells to-day
    Has told the truth my verse now tells;
"We will be true"—How sweet their lay!
        The music of the bells.

For in our heart a charm there dwells,
All doubting fear with power to allay,
The might of Love, that all compels.

In sunshine and in storm to obey
All his behests, and then there dwells
Perennial joy, and still will stay
        The music of the bells.

Sonnets.

HOME.

1.—YOUTH.

BLEST word! thou dost recall the dearest place
  Our hearts have ever known or lov'd; where we,
  In childhood's years long past, so glad and free,
  Could ever find that smiling love-lit face
Of mother, in whose sheltering warm embrace
  Our childish griefs were hush'd so peacefully
  To rest. In her fond love we seem'd to see
  That love, which time nor death can e'er efface.
O memories dear to hearts cast down and tried!
  Ye come like gentle breezes from above,
  To cool our aching brow at eventime,
And fill us with a longing deep to hide
  Within the arms of Everlasting love
  The cares and sorrows of our manhood's prime.

HOME.

2.—MANHOOD.

SING on, sweet bird, thy heart-outpouring lay!
  Whence come those thrilling tones, we know full well;
The praise of that snug nest, thy home, they tell,
  And of thy mate, still dearer day by day.
O happy birds and blessed hearts! when they,
  Who build the nest, with love's own raptures swell;
Beneath its hallowed beams content they dwell,
  And make their home a heaven on earth alway.
The world's mad din in echoes faint they hear;
  Its empty joys they heed not, nor its frown;
For its sad griefs they shed a willing tear,
And yield a helping hand; while for their own,
  Home hath an oil and wine of potence rare,
  Love's healing balm, to soothe each grief and care.

HOME.

3.—OLD AGE.

O WEARY ones, with hearts bereav'd and sore!
    For you how precious are the peace and rest
Which home can give, when ye have strength no more
    To wage the fight of life, while in the west
Your sun is slowly sinking! Then how blest
    If, as in memory oft ye ponder o'er
    Life's varied pages, on some faithful breast
Ye lean, while those "not lost, but gone before"
Come back and smile as in some waking dream;
    And past and present seem but one, and ye
At times are longing for the last long sleep,
Which knows but peace, and, as ye truly deem,
    Will give back your belov'd, from partings free,
    In that bright Home on high, where none may weep.

THE LABOURERS' HIRE.

O MASTER! what for us shall be the "hire"?
    Dare we indeed the end anticipate?
  We, who for Thee began to work so late,
  Or we who, working longer, often tire,
Or work not with a willing heart's desire?
    Wilt Thou our feeble hands compassionate,
    And our imperfect deeds with Thine so great
  Amend; and with Thy love cleanse as with fire?
Then may we still toil on, though weak our heart,
    Though, faint and weary, oft our spirits quail,
    Still striving each to do our little part:
The wish'd-for rest, we know shall never fail,
    When Thou, as evening shadows gently fall,
    Shalt bid, the labourers from the vineyard call.

"THEY SUPPOSED THEY SHOULD HAVE RECEIVED MORE."

FOND thought, still haunting many a faithful heart
   Which in the vineyard serve the Saviour Lord,
   And, in obedience to His blessed word,
Strives to fulfil the God-appointed part.
How natural on such a task to start
   With high anticipations of success,
   Aims which we feel our Lord will largely bless,
Then falter under disappointment's smart.
What strange presumption, pride, and fantasy!
   For what desert have e'en our bravest strife,
   Our costliest sacrifice, our largest dole?
Enough, if ours the promised gift may be
   To share Thy lot, O Lord, who gave Thy life
   To save from utter loss each thankless soul.

                        A. P. P. C., *March*, 1887.

NOTE.—The Author of the above Sonnet, the Dean of York, kindly gives me permission to insert it here; interesting as being suggested by the same parable as the preceding one, and of value for its intrinsic worth.

SATURDAY EVENING.

THE six days' work for hard-earn'd daily bread
    Is done, and round the humble cottage fire
  Creeps evening peace, in loving hearts to inspire
  That heaven-sent joy, which of content is bred.
O'er all outside the village homes is spread
    A calm, as on the upward-pointing spire
    Of lowly Church, in silence all entire,
  We gaze; and, as amid the graves we tread,
The unsaid thought of love seems converse meet
    With those at rest around the house of prayer.
    O, holy ones! are ye not with us still
In peaceful home, in bustling mart and street,
    To help us all our daily cross to bear,
    For Sabbath morn our heart with joy to fill?

DANTE'S "VITA NUOVA."

O NOBLE suffering soul, here may we know,
    And in our hearts the throbs of thine may feel,
  Before it bled with wounds time could not heal!
  In Beatrice's eyes, Love thee did shew
That blest new life of love in youth's first glow—
    So deep, so pure, so strong, that thou could'st kneel,
  As if to saint divine thou would'st reveal
  The veneration of an ardent vow.
And yet in Beatrice's eyes all bliss
    For thee, for us, we know can ne'er be found;
  So when our heart's deep yearning would renew
Youth's glorious fervour, we so sadly miss,
    Turn we, like thee, to Love which knows no bound,
  For Heaven's best gift, a life for ever new.

DURHAM CATHEDRAL.

O VISION grand! 'twere surely no surprise
 To know this house of God from heaven had come,
Descending from the far-off azure skies,
 To grace this spot of earth, a very home
For souls devout; and that on angel's plume
 'Twill leave in sight of our enraptur'd eyes
 This beauteous hill, when sounds the trump of doom
That calls earth's waiting sleepers to arise.
As in this lovely vale we take our way,
 And gaze in wonder on these graceful towers,
 So fairly gleaming in the light of day,
Do they not seem to speak to heart of ours,
 And raise our lagging thoughts from things terrene
 To the great jasper-city walls serene!

TO THE PRIMROSE.

FAIR flower, so dear in childhood's joyous time!
    To look on thee, and thy sweet breath inhale,
  Like magic wand can take us to the vale
  Where all the woodland banks in spring's fresh
      prime
With thee were bright; while in their notes sublime
    The songsters told thy praise, until the dale
    Seem'd likest Paradise, beyond the veil
  That hides the home to which our thoughts
      would climb!
Thou pale, meek flower! O teach our wayward
      heart
    Again to seek the peace it once did know,
    Ere yet earth's stains had soiled its garments
      fair;
When, sweet as is thy scent, it could impart
    A fervent love, all beauteous with the glow
    Of truth, and pure as childhood's lisping prayer.

THE SILVER WEDDING.

O HAPPY souls, in love long-tried and well!
   What joy, as on the years long past ye gaze,
   To find in life's oft dark, perplexing ways,
   Yourselves still closer bound by love's own spell!
O blessed home, the heart's strong citadel,
   Upon whose altar burns no dazzling blaze,
   But love's own fire, to warm with glowing rays
   Those hearts, that oft with grateful gladness swell!
And now, as auburn turns to silver'd gray,
   While hand in hand ye tread life's downward slope,
   Still cheering, strengthening each along the way,
May the bright bow of God's eternal hope
   Beam o'er you, till shall set life's westering sun,
   And ye shall hear the welcome words "Well done!"

CONSTANCY.

THEY wander'd thro' the oft-frequented vale,
    Where, in their childhood's days so blest and free,
    Time sped on gladsome wings of mirth and glee;
    And where one evening, 'neath the moonbeams pale,
She listen'd, trembling, to the oft-told tale
    Of love; and in her heart she vow'd that he
    Should find, in truest love and constancy,
    That she for him thro' all would never fail.
And now draws gently on the eve of life,
    When, after the fierce glare of noontide heat,
    And all the bitter blasts of this world's scorn,
They still trudge on as loving man and wife,
    At times with drooping hands and wearied feet,
    Yet looking for the Everlasting Morn.

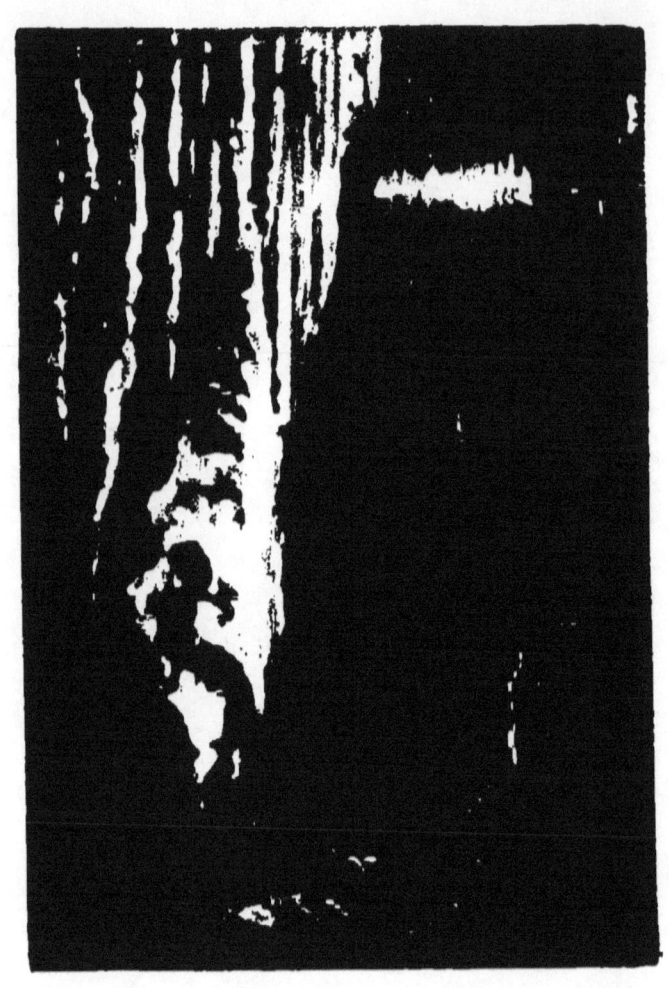

VOICES OF THE SEA.

MY lonely course was by the heaving sea,
   Whose waves made music for my troubled soul;
I heard those voices 'mid their sullen roll
Which here on earth no more shall speak with me!
And tones there were of deep solemnity;—
   The knell of buried hopes they seem'd to toll,
   That once with joy could all my heart control,
But now, alas! lie dead in calm serenity.
O buried hopes! O hearts that beat no more!
   I listen to the wailings of the deep,
   Which now in restless mournful beatings toss,
Until upon this pleasant moonlit shore
   My burthen'd heart hath moan'd itself to sleep,
   To rest for ever 'neath my Saviour's cross.

ABSENCE.

MY sweetest love, how oft of thee I think!
    On morning's earliest beams I hie away
  In thought upon thy breast my head to lay,
  Where oft from love's own lips I fondly drink
His godlike nectar; and when comes day's brink,
    And I am weary of life's fight and fray,
    How sweet, as falls the quiet evening gray,
  In musings of thy love all ills to sink!
O love, how dark, without thy cheering light,
    The lives in fretful toil we wear out here!
    But when, like morning's sun, all clear and bright
Upon our troubled lot thou dost appear,
    Our toil shines fair as with celestial rays,
    Calm falls our even and joy crowns our days.

"TO-DAY SHALT THOU BE WITH ME IN PARADISE."

WITH Thee to be in Paradise to-day,
    O gentle soul! The afterwards for me,
    When from the world my guilty soul should flee,
    All dark and hopeless loom'd; but now a ray
So bright hath beam'd, I cast my fears away,
    And all the tortures of the dreaded tree
    Are sooth'd, while now my soul may rest on Thee,
    And gazing thus would ever by Thee stay.
O shameful deed! to torture thus that frame
    So worn! Those tender hands raised but to bless!
    My God! can this be then a sacrifice,
And Thy great love untold the altar flame?
    But see! He dies, and I am in distress,
    Until with Him I rest in Paradise.

EASTER EVEN.

THE last dread conflict o'er, Thou art at rest!
    Thy bitter foes, their vengeance wreak'd,
        are gone;
Thy dear ones, weeping, lonely, all undone,
Have laid Thee gently down on earth's cold
        breast,
Where for awhile Thy wounded heart is blest
    With peace, such peace as Thou for us hath won,
    When all life's trials o'er, its day's work done,
    Weary and weak, we crave a little rest.
O Saviour dear! when on our aching heart
    The world's sad evil ways so darkly press,
    And sin and grief becloud the path we tread,
Help Thou us then with Thee to go apart,
    Stand by Thy grave, and know the blessedness
    Of conquer'd self, and sin in Thee laid dead.

EASTER DAY.

O GLORIFIED! death's bonds asunder burst,
   With alleluias loud we hail Thee free,
While Heaven resounds with songs of victory!
With trembling faith Thy lovéd ones scarce durst
Believe the blessed truth, that Thou should'st first
   Bow Thy meek head in woe to death's decree,
   And then for evermore to us should'st be
The mighty Victor of our foe accurst!
O joyous day! The dreadful night is past!
   And Hope in glorious Easter beams all bright
   Can see, beyond earth's parting pangs so drear,
Those meetings, which she knows will come at last,
   When dawns the Easter-day that hath no night,
   And God Himself doth wipe away each tear.

BY THE SEA-SHORE.

WITH hearts that beat in unison, we went
    Along the margin of the summer sea,
Whose glancing waves seem'd full of joyous
    glee,
And of their gladness to our hearts they lent.
The evening's calm, our spirit's sweet content,
    Spread o'er the beauteous scene all peacefully
    The precious rest so full of hope, which we,
    To bless our souls, deem'd Heaven itself had
        sent.
No vocal hymn of thanks our voices sung,
    And yet more grateful hearts than ours that
        eve
Ne'er moved to joyous tones a willing tongue;
And He who knows all thoughts, we can believe,
    From our full hearts ask'd not for words, or
        more
    Than waves' sweet praises by that pleasant
        shore.

CALLED AWAY.

"RISE up, my love, my fair one, come away;"
    The wintry sky, poor dove, is sad and drear;
For thee shall beam a far serener day,
    Beneath My smile the sky is bright and clear.
Thy tender yearnings, and thy love sincere,
    That crave with mourning hearts a longer stay,
    Leave thou with Me; and I will bring them here
    "When day shall break and shadows flee away."
Come, then, my dove, and rest thy pinions weak,
    Refreshment sweet for thy poor weary heart,
    Reward have I for patient love and meek,
So tired with earth's sad toil and bitter smart;
    For thee here rest eternal shall begin:
"Then He put forth His hand and took her in."

TO THE DEPARTED.

YE dear departed ones, in God's peace blest,
   Whose forms we laid beneath earth's sheltering sod,
  Or which 'neath ocean's waves the trump of God
Await, that calls to everlasting rest:
How with those mortal frames, which did invest
  Your love when side by side with us ye trod
  Life's path, ye have laid by each soiling clod
Of imperfection on your mother's breast!
O death! how sweet their memories thou dost keep;
  Their love for us for evermore is sure,
  Free from earth's change. So let them rest awhile,
Till in life's eve we, too, would fall asleep,
  To wake and find our lovéd ones all pure,
  And glorified beneath our Father's smile.

CHRISTMAS.

FAIR Babe that smil'st from lowly manger-
bed,
  To Thee we bring each heart-inspiring lay,
  While round each love-blest hearth this home-
lov'd day
  Are gladly gather'd dear ones, hither led
By tenderest ties; and hearts that oft have bled
  Are sooth'd and heal'd; and dear ones far away
  In spirit arms are fondly clasp'd, till they
  Smile too with us in beams from Bethlehem
shed.
Bring carol quaint or hymn devout that tells
  The gladsome joys of happy Christmas-tide,
  And as o'er all the land the clanging bells
Resound, and spread the message far and wide,
  Even sadden'd hearts shall feel the joy that
dwells
  Where lowly love with Bethlehem's babe doth
bide.

THE CHRISTMAS BELLS.

YE happy bells, your voices sweet and clear
    Again with our home-gladden'd hearts keep time,
And in your joyous tones we seem to hear
    That blest angelic choral song sublime!
As on your wings of praise on high we climb,
    Ye call us each to lay aside all fear;
And while we list your merry clanging chime,
    To leave the cares that often vex us here!
O happy hearts, as now in tune to-day,
    Once more ye learn the old story ever new;
Shed forth on all around the cheering light
Of smiling love, and in your deeds allay
    Some pangs of want and pain, that thus for you
    The Christmas bells may tell their tale aright.

MORNING.

HAIL, beauteous morn! How fair each early beam!
   Lead on thine hours in brightening, glad array,
   And as the rising lark salutes the day
   Let grateful hearts take up the joyous theme;
While far and near, o'er hill and sparkling stream,
   Melodious wake the tuneful songsters gay,
   As joyful thus they would their matins say,
   And hymn their bounteous Maker's praise supreme.
Come, then, dear heart, be heard no murmuring voice;
   Away with fears that peace of mind destroy.
   Shall we, too, not with all around rejoice?
For us all nature wakes again with joy;
   Now make we duty's path our glorious choice,
   And there our willing hands find meet employ.

JOHN BUNYAN.

"And after that they shut up the gates, which when I had seen I wished myself among them."—Pilgrim's Progress.

O WONDROUS dreamer, with thy power divine,
  How all our pilgrim-life thy dream hath told—
  Our load of sin, our hopes, our doubts so cold,
  The fearful battle with the foe malign;
And Beulah's beauteous land, where none repine,
  We long to see; we dare with joy "be bold,"
  While we with thee in living faith behold
  The New Jerusalem on high to shine.
When, as thy gaze beyond the gates did pass,
  Which open'd wide to let thy pilgrims in,
    And thou didst feast thine eyes, oft filled with tears,
Well may we feel that thou could'st wish, alas!
  That thou had'st done with this world's care and sin,
    To rest amid that throng for endless years.

In Memoriam.

Dr. J. P. BELL, of Hull.

BESIDE the grave a voice fell on mine ear,
   Which told of peace eternal, and of "rest
From labour" 'mid the glories of the blest!
Sweet words of comfort to the lov'd and dear!
Your Father wipes away the trembling tear.
   O leave your lov'd one on his Saviour's breast,
   Who call'd him hence to peace; He knoweth best
When for us all to end our labour here.
O gracious soul, who here with us didst tread
   The path so clearly marked by virtues three!
   We doubt not, in that glorious lodge on high,
Our Master all thy wish doth gratify
   In fullest light of immortality,
   And for thy works the words "Well done!" hath said.

P

THE RISING MOON.

COME forth, O queen, in radiant beauty fair!
    Unveil, and beam thy spirit-soothing light,
Thou calm, majestic empress of the night!
And while my soul is freed from clouds of care,
And seeks thy undisturbéd peace to share,
    O let me rest awhile from earth's drear fight,
    And mount on spirit-wings unto the height
Where reigns Heaven's bliss without impair!
How sweet, when all the toils of day are o'er,
    On pure devotion's wings to rise, and leave
    Behind awhile each heavy earthly cross,
To seek new strength of heart, and patience more
    In loving trust to wait and to receive
    His peace, to which all earthly gain is loss.

LOVE'S FEAST.

"Can the children of the Bridechamber fast while the Bridegroom is with them?"

How could they fast while Thou, their Lord divine,
  Before their faint and hungering souls didst spread
  Thy bounteous feast of love, which, as they fed,
  Seem'd manna, angels' food and choicest wine?
Such precious words fell from those lips of Thine,
  Like honey, while Thy loving eyes did shed
  Such joy that all life's fears are fled.
  Not now they fast, but feast on food divine!
But now the Bridegroom's voice we hear no more,
  And we must fast as through the desert drear
  We journey on, content with foretaste meet
Enough for pilgrim-needs, our daily store,
  Till at the Supper of the Lamb we hear
  The Bridegroom's voice His bride in glory greet.

www.ingramcontent.com/pod-product-compliance
Lightning Source LLC
Chambersburg PA
CBHW020104170426
43199CB00009B/391